Donal Nea

Pilgrim 2000

Easter 2000

the columba press

First published in 2000 by
the columba press
55A Spruce Avenue, Stillorgan Industrial Park,
Blackrock, Co Dublin

Cover by Bill Bolger
Origination by The Columba Press
Printed in Ireland by Colour Books Ltd, Dublin

ISBN 1 85607 293 2

Preface

Each season of the year has its doorway to prayer, its themes of the mystery of Jesus' life. Advent involves us in the birth of Jesus, and Lent, in his suffering and death, and engages us also in these mysteries in human life, for prayer and life are one.

Easter is our introduction to Jesus who consoles, who calls us to belong to him and to take part in his worldwide mission of love. As he himself was raised to new life from death, he invites us to share in that life and share it.

Our themes for Easter 2000 introduce us to these different mysteries of the activity of Jesus in the themes of Openings, Closures, Shadows, Streams, Belonging, Mission, and Love. Some are images of resurrection which hint at different meanings of our sharing now in the life of the risen Lord. Others touch on realities of life which are part of a Christian's following of the risen Jesus. All are part of the mystery of Jesus' risen life and our unity with him. Thus they are part of the mystery of our lives, for prayer and life are one.

The empty tomb opened the eyes of the disciples to a radically new life, and like all openings, some closures of the past would be involved. The old Jesus, and ways of looking on things, has gone, or has been integrated into the new: our first two weeks.

Shadows, all caused by the sun, and streams refreshing and creative, are images of the risen life of Jesus, for his risen light is what causes shadows which protect, enclose and guard our ways. These images may speak to us of the risen Lord.

As an effect of the resurrection, we belong to Jesus in the community of the church. We are partners with him in his work in the world to bring forth the kingdom of God. We are invited to receive the love of God and share in this love.

The resurrection of Jesus is his life now and forever. In his risen life he has been our inspiration and encouragement through the almost 2000 years since his death. Our text however refers little to Jubilee, for the sake of some variety from the other booklets of this series, but the themes of Easter 2000 take up the themes of our Jubilee spirituality – joy, reconciliation, justice, gratitude, and witness.

Easter 2000 may be used for personal reflection as a sort of 'Thought for the Day', or may be a reflection for shared prayer. The Jesus of our prayer is always the risen Lord; thus the prayer of Easter invites us to read his life, and live our own lives, in the shadow of the resurrection, in the stream of the living water and always from this side of Easter.

Donal Neary SJ

Easter Sunday AN OPEN DOOR

There's a welcome to an open door. You pass by and maybe feel someone wants you to come in – someone may be waiting. An open door is like a heart open in welcome. The open door to the tomb of Jesus is something like that. We may be fearful initially but it's an invitation from God to join in the risen life of Jesus. It's a strange welcome – when you go in, there is nobody there. The host is gone, but not absent, for the welcome invites you outwards, and you find the trace and fragance of Jesus, not only in the tomb, but in the new home of the risen Lord, everywhere. In the risen Lord, God is found everywhere and in everything.

Lord, may I find you
in all the experiences of life,
in all the events of life.

Monday of the 1st Week of Easter YOUR CLOTHES AND HIS!

Picture for a moment the tomb of Jesus. On the floor are the clothes which were put on him after death and anointing by Mary and his friends. These are rolled up, no longer used. They had covered a blood-stained body and shrouded him in the love of his mother like swaddling clothes at Bethlehem. And look again in your imagination. See your own clothes beside his clothes, festive or ordinary. Your clothes beside his – a sign of the closeness of your friendship with the risen Lord. He has gone on his mission and invites you to join him. Surprising what you find beyond an open door!

Lord, thank you for friendship,
for sharing the journey of life,
for sharing your call to life.

Tuesday of the 1st Week of Easter RISEN IN THE EARTH

The earth has opened to receive the body of God. Earth – the place of secret growth, of the hidden mysteries of time and creation, receiving the one in whom all was created. Earth received Jesus during his life – the ground offered rest on his journeys, and the caves of the desert welcomed him at his times of testing, offering space for his calling and convictions to grow. The deep waters of the Jordan received him into the beginnings of humanity, for in our beginnings we are all surrounded by water. He spoke of trees and fields and seeds to preach the word. The womb of the earth received him, and like a mother opens to give him back to the people of the earth.

Jesus, friend of the earth, enliven us.
Jesus, in whom the world is created, encourage us.
Jesus, in whom the world holds its being, sustain us.

Wednesday of the 1st Week of Easter NEW WORLD

A good piece of music or a beautiful work of art may open a door to thoughts and feelings otherwise untapped. The resurrection of the Lord is something like that. As the stone was rolled back from the tomb, a new world was created. The Word of God, in whom all has been created, creates a new world within us and among us. The door is opened to a world of reconciliation, justice, peace, compassion and care. We are ministers, servants, of the resurrection, and Easter happens today because of Jesus' followers. We have the key to open the door of Easter, entrusted to us by Jesus. Without faithful followers, the resurrection of Jesus remains like words on paper; with his followers the word comes to life.

Lord, you are the door to new life,
the key to that door,
may we share this life among us.

Thursday of the 1st Week of Easter NEW PRESENCE

Some people have a sort of presence in a room. A man or woman may communicate an angry presence or a loving presence just by being there, not even saying anything. Or a child may bring a presence of fun into a room. Or with some people we feel a security by their presence. The risen Jesus brings a new presence to the world. Just be being alive in his risen life and body, he makes the world a more secure place, and a more challenging place. His presence, in prayer and in love, sacrament and scripture, bring consolation to the disturbed, and disturb the comfortable. The Christian lives in the atmosphere of joy and security, consolation and comfort, in good times and bad.

Jesus, consoler, be close to us,
Jesus, friend, be close to us,
Risen Lord, may we spread your gospel.

Friday of the 1st Week of Easter LAUGHTER

There are some people whose company is like an open door to laughter. Always a joke, a funny word, and happiness around them. They are people who can laugh with tears or through tears. They seem to have a knack of lifting spirits and of enabling others to appreciate the good of life. Jesus' resurrection is something like that. His presence among us now is an open door to joy: that there is always hope, always something to be grateful for, and that he is present among us for all time. The risen Lord is close to us in every experience of our lives so that we can find something of the peace and joy of God in our lives. Light-heartedness, fun and the joy that can be found in trouble, are all moments of resurrection.

Jesus, you are joy to the full,
you are the joy of God,
be joy in each of us.

Saturday of the 1st Week of Easter ILLNESS

There are openings in sickness. Illness is a teacher, unwelcome and uninvited. But it is part of everyone's life and can make us better people. It can also make us bitter. Only the person who is ill knows the lessons of illness, and it is unhelpful for anyone to try to say what illness might teach us. Nobody wants to hear platitudes like, 'God never closes one door but he opens another', or 'You're never given illness without the grace to bear it'. Our best gift to a person who is ill is our presence and gentle support while illness teaches its own lessons. Only I can answer the question for myself, 'What has your illness taught you?' When I have answered it, even briefly, I may be able to listen to another.

Lord, always a friend, be with us,
Lord, strength of the weak, comfort us,
Lord, comfort of the sick, strengthen us.

Sunday of the 2nd Week of Easter THE MYSTERY OF OUR FAITH

Faith is a strange reality. We almost expect its path to be smooth – some thing we 'get' at birth or baptism and it will sustain us always. Like any relationship, it goes through its doubts, questions, darkness times, as well as its times of peace, joy and exhilaration. At times it seems intensely personal, almost private, but we know that faith grows in each through the faith of others. There are times when we know from the inside of our experience the words of Jesus to Thomas: 'Happy are those who have not seen but believe.' We may expect that faith will be tested and tried by life and by routine, by God and others. Is reality the best word for faith? It seems to be more a mystery than a reality, a hand to be held rather than a problem to be solved.

Lord, I believe, help my faith.
Lord, I believe, strengthen my faith.
Lord, I believe, help me share my faith.

Monday of the 2nd Week of Easter LETTING GO

We let go of adolescence to enter adulthood, childhood to enter adolescence. The process of letting go in life is continuous, as every stage of our growing involves shedding something of the past. Marriage means the opening of the door to the future with a certain closing on other relationships, even with our own family. Another family will become more central in our lives. Closings are frightening for many people. There's the fear of losing something we value and enjoy, and we need the courage to know that the future can always be better. The last closure of all – death – is the open door to a new life. This is the risen life of Jesus, the resurrection he dared to hope for and give his life for.

Lord Jesus, be our courage in tough times,
our hope in times of fear,
love always.

Tuesday of the 2nd Week of Easter BREAKING WAVES

As a wave moves towards the shore, we know that it will break. Much of our lives, like the waves, have their breaking points. Stress, frustration, disappointment, loss are all part of life. At times we almost break like the wave on the shore. And the wave returns, bringing what it found on the shore with it. We break, but every breaking point is a growth point. At every point of hurt is the chance of deeper love and freedom, in every loss is the chance to find something new. Every breaking point can point out new resources in a person. Even bereavement, the loss of someone dear, can be a door opening to living out of new strengths. This is risen life.

Lord, in the closing
of every treasured door in my life,
let me believe in the chance of deeper life.

Wednesday of the 2nd Week of Easter PAINFUL CLOSURES

Some closures in life are painful and at such a time people need the support of friends and of a community like the church. Separations in marriage cause a mixture of pain and relief, as does the change or break-up of any commitment. There are feelings of disappointment and betrayal – when people make a commitment like marriage, priesthood or religious life, they hope it will last and grow and bring life. The church may present an uncompassionate face at times of break-up or change. There is a call, a need and a hope for all in the church that we can see beyond externals to the reasons people made new decisions, and a challenge to show at all times the compassionate face of the risen Lord.

Lord, may we share your risen life
in understanding others
and in our efforts to understand in times of conflict.

Thursday of the 2nd Week of Easter BURNT ASHES

There is a closure in the burning of the palms on Palm Sunday. What were used to honour Jesus in a sense lost their life. Ashes point to something final, like when we burn a body. Yet these ashes are retained and will be used again at the beginning of another cycle of death and resurrection, as they will be used for the following Ash Wednesday. Can we see this as a statement that nothing is ever final in the context of God and of Jesus Christ? Burnt ashes will give life again, and even the burnt human body will rise to new life, anointed and youthful to enjoy the life and vision of God forever.

Jesus, bringer of life, be with us.
Jesus, bringer of hope, be with us.
Jesus, always love and friend, be with us.

Friday of the 2nd Week of Easter AN END TO POVERTY

Wouldn't we hope to close the door on poverty, war, injustice of all kinds, violence, abuse? Our hope is for a closure of the human suffering caused by greed for money and power, by class snobbery, religious intolerance, and all the different ways in which we make each other suffer. Could we find tombs for poverty and violence, and close the door so that it could never again be opened? This is a God-given hope and a Jesus-given desire. It is the atmosphere of the risen Lord, and the call to each Christian is to be a minister of the resurrection – to do our bit to close these doors of suffering and open the door of the risen Lord. None of us is the cause of all the suffering of the world, but each of us can be part of the solution.

Lord Jesus, work in me.
Lord Jesus, love in me.
Lord Jesus, die and rise in me.

Saturday of the 2nd Week of Easter LETTING HURT GO

When we let a hurt go, there's a new freedom. We can harbour a grudge for years and it festers in us. We see or think of a person, and feel heavy, angry, frustrated. If we let go, that burden is gone. If we forgive in one relationship, we walk more freely in other relationships also. Healing of past hurts happens in honest prayer, in conversation with the person concerned if possible, and with good friends, maybe with some counselling. Sometimes we can see the reasons why someone did what was done, and it helps. We need to desire this freedom, and really want to let the grudge go. We also need patience with our letting-go; forgiveness takes time. It is human to feel hurt and anger and bear grudges; but it is also in the power of the human being to let go. Be grateful for grudges that have been let go.

Lord Jesus, you are the healer of hurts.
You are peace on earth.
You are compassion to everyone.

Sunday of the 3rd Week of Easter LIGHTS AND SHADOWS

Maybe shadow is a strange image for the resurrection. But when you think of it, shadows are caused by light. Light shining through a tree gives its shadow, and shadows give space from too much sun. The resurrection of Jesus is the light in which we live. The shade of the resurrection is our environment of life. It is the light within much of the drabness and even darkness of human living. We live in the darkness of violence, poverty, hurt, disillusion, and through it all shines the light of the risen Lord. We are people of the light who live in the shadow of his death; and his death is the beginning of light and life.

Be hope, Lord Jesus, in distress,
be light in darkness,
be love always.

Monday of the 3rd Week of Easter UNIQUE IN JESUS

'She lived in her sister's shadow' – this means that she was possibly seen only in relation to a more accomplished sister. All of us want to live our own lives and be our own person. We don't want to be accepted only for our family name or wealth or reputation. We want to be seen by others as unique and individual. This is the way God sees us. Living our lives in the shadow of Jesus doesn't take away this uniqueness. God 'can see and love in us what he sees and loves in Jesus' without us losing ourselves. In the light of Jesus we see ourselves in our true identity, loved children of God our Father. It's a bit like the Trinity – they live in each other and are three distinct Persons. In Jesus we live too and are our own person.

Lord, make us one;
with you in me and I in you,
may the world know your grace.

Tuesday of the 3rd Week of Easter THE SHADOW OF DEATH

We often say that we live our lives in the shadow of death. It's a realistic image. We know the harshness of death, and its certainty in life. We know our fears of death and our dread that an illness may precede our death. Death's shadow is in the light of the resurrection. We have ways of saying this – 'life is changed, not ended'; and by this we mean that the shadow of death 'gives way to the bright promise of immortality'. The light of the resurrection causes the shadow, which is the shadow of death. We are people of a path bathed in light, like a road which is brightened in spots by light coming through trees and clouds.

Lord, be with us,
light in any shadows,
now and at the hour of our death.

Wednesday of the 3rd Week of Easter SHADOW SELF

Bits of the good in the worst of us and bits of the bad in the best of us – an old saying. There's a shadow side to all of us – the self we don't like, our faults and failings. And there are the good qualities, talents, good desires and the good we do for others. Every good quality has a sort of fault that goes with it – a person with a quick temper is often very generous, a lazy person often very peace-making; a person bound on success may open the way for jobs for many others. We are a mixture of darkness and brightness, shadows and lights. The light of God may grow brighter in us as we grow older, as we pray and share our life of faith with others. Our faults lessen as we nourish our virtues and the light is brighter than any darkness.

Lord, Jesus, light of the world,
be light for me, be light in me,
be light for others through me.

Thursday of the 3rd Week of Easter SHADOWS OF POWER

Most of us are not powerful publicly. But we have power as parents, religious, voters, teachers, to work for the good of people and a new generation. Power can be a light for the world, or the shadow that keeps others in darkness. Humanity has the power to ensure that sometime Zambia will no longer crippled by world debt, that every street-child in Calcutta will be educated and fed. Power can be used as a light for others, or as a way of oppression. The power of Jesus was never for himself, always to heal, comfort and make life better for others. His risen life is this sort of power. His was the power of service, using what influence and authority he had to better the lives of others and bring them to God.

Lord Jesus, gentle in power,
powerful in your gentleness,
may we work in service for you.

Friday of the 3rd Week of Easter LIGHT AT THE CENTRE

There is a centre in each of us which is the source of our goodness; it is the place and space of God, within which God makes a home. We can journey to that centre, like the centre of the universe, and there we find our real self. It is the light of self, and the light of God dwelling within us. It's like walking a road through the shadows and the lights: parts of the path bathed in light, other parts shadowed by trees from the brightness of the sun. And then we come out of shadows into light, as happens if we find that centre of ourselves where we are timeless, loved, and part of God. It is the space within ourselves where all the love of our lives is housed. This is the risen Lord within each of us.

Lord, you are at the centre of my being;
attract me there, invite me there,
finding you in the depths of my being.

Saturday of the 3rd Week of Easter DREAM OF LIGHT

The Christian dream is to be light-bearers. In the space of ourselves where God dwells, lives the word of God, calling us into his service. We may think we can do little. We may think that the work of God today requires experts. The work of God is built on love and cannot last without love. Otherwise all our works, no matter how good and how much centred on the gospel, are only projects. The Christian dream is to be a light bearer wherever we go, and to whoever we meet. To give the gift of human dignity to a dying person was the life dream of Mother Teresa, and her dream was a Christian dream, for the basic Christian belief is that everyone matters equally to God. Our dream is to share that light of God with everyone, and for that we need, not a professional degree, but a strong love, a love that wants to share.

Risen Jesus, here I am,
willing to do what I can
in your service.

Sunday of the 4th Week of Easter STREAMS OF LIFE

The stream nourishes the roots in its vicinity. Food, flowers, all that grows, needs water. The resurrection of Jesus can be glimpsed in many images. It's like a stream giving life to all it touches. The risen life of Jesus is not bound to time or space; it's the life of God giving life to all. Somehow it gets blocked without our co-operation. Jesus entrusts his life now to us, and this is a huge act of trust. We are the word of God and the compassion of God, the justice of God and the care of God today. He believes in us enough to entrust his risen life to us. We pray to hold that trust sincerely and live by it.

Lord Jesus, life of the world,
you have entrusted your life to us;
make us live by that trust.

Monday of the 4th Week of Easter CONSOLING WATERS

A name for Jesus after the resurrection is 'consoler'. An old tradition has him visiting his mother first after the resurrection, with a presence and message of consolation for her. The presence of Jesus is intensely personal, reaching deep down into our personality where each of us finds our unique personality. Within all the hopes and dreams, sin and sorrow, love and hate of our lives, is the space of ourselves which is the soul of ourselves. That mystery of the human being, body and soul, which is timeless, is the dwelling place of God. The consolation of Jesus reaches deep down to our uniqueness. His challenge is to share that consolation with others.

Jesus, consoler, be our joy.
Jesus, our joy, be our peace.
Jesus, our peace, may we be peacemakers.

Tuesday of the 4th Week of Easter UNDERGROUND WATERS

A map sometimes shows an underground stream. Or a stream may be known in the memories of people who lived on the land. Only when you know the place do you know the stream is there. Our image of the resurrection like a stream of life has its 'underground moments'. On the surface, life can seem troubled, distressed and you feel you're going through a really bad time. Bereavement and loss of many kinds, illness, depression, are dark times. The stream of God's love may seem intangible and you don't know if it still exists. The peace once so close seems far away or gone. Even then, the risen life of Jesus is part of the mystery of our life, and it's like an underground stream. Unseen, unknown at times, but still the risen Lord does his work of consoling, of friendship and always with the promise of hope.

Lord, hope in darkness,
consolation in loss,
be with us now and always.

Wednesday of the 4th Week of Easter PEACEFUL WATERS

Streams can be peaceful places. You just sit there and the sound of the water calms you, bringing peace and relaxation. Jesus says to all he meets after the resurrection, 'Peace be with you.' This is his continuous gift. We know the joy of finding peace of mind and heart after failures, tensions, times of danger and hurt. Just as the sound of a stream gradually brings its peace, our relationship with Jesus gives the peace that comes 'dropping slow'. It is a deep and lasting peace in the mind and heart. Its source is prayer, friendship and living a life in harmony with the gospel of Jesus.

Lord, giver of peace,
make us channels of your peace,
people of light in darkness.

Thursday of the 4th Week of Easter GUSHING WATERS

There are times when the stream breaks out into rushing water, fast-flowing, maybe a waterfall. The living water has its moments of exuberance and of joy. The life, death and resurrection of Jesus has been a source of joy for the years coming to this Jubilee. It has given deep joy to people at times of happiness and sadness. Even in the times which were very rough, there can be a joy deep down which is the joy of the risen Jesus. The stream has become an exuberant pool, or a river which spreads over its banks, breaking boundaries as the resurrection invites us to break the barriers of prejudice, fatalism and of despair. Then we look on all of life from this side of Easter.

Lord Jesus, in your risen life,
be freedom within us, and joy,
be forgiveness and hope.

Friday of the 4th Week of Easter LIVING WATER

'Living water' is a word and image for the gift of Jesus now to the world. It is a name for the Holy Spirit, an intimate way in which Jesus lives among us. In mysterious ways, God gives this Spirit to each of us at baptism. We are welcomed into a community where words like peace, joy, enthusiasm, forgiveness, gentleness, justice, are words to speak in hope and, even more, to live by. The living water is like a word echoing within us or a song in our hearts. We are people of the water, people of the Son of God, people of the Spirit of God. And that Spirit lives within each of us. This is one reason for loving ourselves and each other.

Spirit of the Father and Son, live within us;
Spirit of compassion and love, live within us;
Spirit alive in the world, do good among us.

Saturday of the 4th Week of Easter NOURISHING WATERS

A stream waters the soil around it, and then flows on. The flowers or fruit from the watering will bloom later. You could say the stream will never know the good it did. And it's a bit the same with ourselves. Much good is done which bears its fruit in later years. Parents may wait a long time to see the fruits of their labours and their love; the same with teachers, and with many others in our attempts to help others. Love given is never wasted. Love is like the stream, it waters all around it, and the good results are seen later, or maybe seen somewhere else. The love you give can bear fruit in the way another gives love in later years. No minute of the death of Christ was wasted, because it was given in love, and is all part now of the love of the risen Lord. As he loved in death, he now loves in risen life.

Jesus, consoler of all, be our bringer of joy.
Jesus, comfort of all, be our bringer of peace.
Jesus, friend of all, be our bringer of justice.

Sunday of the 5th Week of Easter ALL BELONG

If we really believe in the resurrection, our attitudes to 'other kinds of people' is radically altered. Our belonging to God in the risen Jesus reaches more deeply within us that the differences which divide us. Differences of colour, nationality, gender, sexual orientation, wealth, education, religion, among many others, can divide. Mostly divisions are fed by fear of the 'other' who in some way threatens our security. The word of the risen Jesus is that all are brothers and sisters, that God has become one of us in death for all, and is raised from death for all. When we hear the real story of a person's life, when differences are heard and there is real communication, our sense of being together as children of God comes to life. We need to 'incarnate' the resurrection of Christ. As we are drawn together in unity by the memory of the birth of Jesus, we can be sustained in unity by our faith in his risen life which calls us all 'brothers and sisters'.

Jesus, living in humanity,
living in the church, living in each person,
bring your people to live in harmony.

Monday of the 5th week of Easter BELONGING TO GOD

Two moments of aloneness are the moment of birth and the moment of death. Even though people may surround us, we are born alone, and we die alone. Nobody can do either for us. We are aware when we think of birth and death that we belong to God. Our deepest belonging is to God, more than to parents, spouse, children, or friend, race or nation. People often say 'when you experience a birth you know God is near', or 'we felt God was around at a death'. In Jesus Christ we have the Son of God born like ourselves, experiencing death like ourselves, and then in his resurrection we believe that our deepest belonging can never be shattered; in his risen life we belong to God.

Jesus, son of the Father, be close to us,
Jesus, word of the Father, speak within us,
Jesus, love of the father, belong to us.

Tuesday of the 5th week of Easter BELONGING IN TRUST

The birth of Jesus, and his death and resurrection, was a statement of God that God belongs to us, as we to God. It is in Jesus we believe this forcefully. When you share deep moments of life with people, you belong to each other in a deep way. Jesus has shared all that is human, and there is no part of our life to which he does not belong. His belonging is the belonging of love. Trusting those we belong to is a reality of our belonging together. Jesus entrusts everything to us. Through prayer, works and the liturgy of the church he belongs to us, and we are his body in the world. Without the people of God, the word cannot be heard, the eucharist cannot be celebrated, the Spirit is quenched. With all our weakness, it is more than amazing that he trusts his message now to us, as God trusted him to Mary and Joseph, and to the faith of his people.

Lord, deepen our belonging in you.
May many belong to you
in our unity with each other.

Wednesday of the 5th week of Easter
BELONGING TO EACH OTHER

At baptism we welcome our children into three families: the family of humanity, the family of the church and the family of birth. It is a celebration of belonging – at a time when a child faces the aloneness of birth and the fear of the first months of life, we say strongly that the child belongs. Belonging in Jesus Christ means we belong to each other. The poet Brendan Kennelly sums it up: 'Self knows that self is not enough.' Belonging is a good feeling, a hunger of the heart, and it is also a responsibility. When we say., 'we belong to each other', we are also saying that we care for each other, just as when Jesus says that he belongs to us, it means that he cares for us.

Lord, you are the centre of our being,
you are the centre of our belonging.
May we exist and belong in you.

Thursday of the 5th week of Easter BELONGING TO THE EARTH
I placed my head on the cross on Good Friday evening. It seemed that I lowered my self onto the wood of Jesus' death, not just my head but all of me. The realisation came over me that Jesus after death 'lowered' himself into the earth. As the cross came from the wood of the earth and was placed in the earth, Jesus in his death became one again with all creation. All was created in him, and after death he would be raised again from the rock of the earth. The earth welcomed him, its creator. We belong to the universe – to the earth, to the people of the earth, to the soil and the streams of earth that give life. The jubilee of Jesus is a sort of jubilee also for the earth and we, of all people, are to be respecters of the earth, for in earth is the risen life of Jesus Christ.
Lord, friend of the earth, be near;
friend of the poor, be near;
risen life of God, be near.

Friday of the 5th week of Easter BELONGING IN JUSTICE
If we belong to each other, we are responsible for the life of each other. As the earth offers its life to everyone, we live by the faith that all are entitled to food, shelter, education, health care, life itself and a way of life that is dignified with the name human. That's behind the hope in the Jubilee year of removing the debts in the developing world, debts that deny ordinary human rights to a population. Our belonging is not just to our own country but to the people of the world, particularly those in greatest need. Belonging means we work for equality, and Christian work is for the dignity and equality of all. This is the prayer of Jesus, the work of Jesus and the will of God.
Lord Jesus, may your kingdom come,
may God's will be done
on earth in every land, near and far.

Saturday of the 5th week of Easter **BEING GRATEFUL**

At any Jubilee there will be statements of gratitude – thanks for belonging to the family, the community, the group or association which celebrates the Jubilee. That's some of the mystery of celebrating the Jubilee of Jesus' life. We can think of the fireworks and the celebration which marked the beginning of the millennium, and associate it all with our thanks. Thanks that we are part of the big mystery and the big mission of Jesus Christ. Thanks that we belong to a group of people which stretches through centuries and continents to make the world a better place. Thanks that we belong to God who never gives up on us, individually or as a people, who is the God of forgiveness, the God of the second chance always, in the death and the resurrection of Jesus Christ.

Lord, be alive in us,
be forgiveness in us.
May we always be grateful.

Sunday of the 6th Week of Easter **MISSION: MEANING IN LIFE**

When the disciples saw the cloths in the tomb they knew that the Lord was raised from death. No longer at rest, he was at work, on mission, finding his disciples so that he could say, 'As the Father sent me, so am I sending you.' A relationship with the risen Lord is a relationship of partnership, of shared mission. We work with him in his daily recreating of love and justice in the world. In faith we know that in our hopes and work for justice, reconciliation, peace and equality, the activity of the risen Lord will be seen and heard today. Our mission with the risen Jesus gives a meaning and direction to our lives which nobody can take from us.

Lord Jesus, be at work for justice among us,
be at work for peace and reconciliation,
be at work always for the dignity of all.

Monday of the 6th Week of Easter MISSION ALWAYS

Bringing freedom to those around us and the world we live in is a sign of the resurrection. Anything that gives a lift of joy and freedom to the heart, or an insight of truth and discovery to the mind, is a mark of the presence of the risen Lord. As ministers of the resurrection, we are, in a sense, always on the job. Not that we are workaholic about our mission; it's just that in everything we do and say, in all the ways we interact with other people, the risen life of Jesus can flow among us. As the scent of a flower interacts with the whole room without the flower doing anything, we can be people of the resurrection by who we are.

Jesus, take this day and all in it;
may my way of being today
be the flow of your risen life.

Tuesday of the 6th Week of Easter MISSION TOGETHER

We were three priests working among teenagers on school retreats. The retreats were good but one-sided. We were all coming from the same place in life and the same type of experience. As years went on the retreat team was mixed – lay, priest, religious, students, men and women. The retreat team was stronger and spoke from a more varied background. This was the beginning of a co-operative ministry in school retreats. The work of Jesus was always done with others and his work now to build the kingdom of God is best done in collaboration. He formed his apostles and disciples to work together. The way forward for the church is in collaboration and co-operation with each other in the work of God.

Gather us to work together, Lord,
to pray together,
and to grow together in your risen life.

Wednesday of the 6th Week of Easter MISSION IN THE WORLD

We look at the needs of the world, then at the gospel and the central strands of Jesus' life. That is how we find out our mission today. Without a relationship with Jesus our mission will scarcely be a Christian mission. Without some awareness of the needs of people in the world today, our mission will scarcely be a Christian mission. Focusing only on the needs of the world may mean a mission of projects and efficiency without compassion; focusing only on Jesus can mean a mission of only prayer and the spiritual, with little reference to loneliness, poverty, injustice and the harshness of the world. Discovering our mission in the world is to journey on the path of ordinary life in the presence of Jesus, risen anew among us.

Lord, grow in each of us,
love in each of us,
make us aware of the needs of your people.

Thursday of the 6th Week of Easter MISSION BLOCKED

Greed, violence, human weakness and selfishness block us from working on the mission of Jesus. The risen Jesus can be almost caged, or nailed again to the cross by the blindness, sin and evil in the world and in the church. We need to know these blocks well. Following on the mission of Jesus means being aware of what may block us in this day and age from hearing the word. Addictions to wealth, power and other addictions guide us along paths where the risen Jesus is hardly recognised. Prejudice and greed and violence nailed Jesus to the cross. The love of God overcame these, as the love of God will raise goodness to life, with Jesus, in the culture of today.

Open our ears to the cries of the world,
open our eyes to the blindness of the world,
open our hearts in trust of your faithfulness.

Friday of the 6th Week of Easter BEING SENT

Once we said Mass at an open door standing, looking out on the place around us, and realised that looking outwards is essential to the eucharist. When we look at the bread at Mass we see the bread broken each day and the wine poured in family, community and friendship. And the bread is broken and the wine is poured, as the lives of many are broken by their suffering, and blood is poured out in the violence and wars of the world. We come from our working with Jesus to the eucharist, and are strengthened to go forward to live as his followers. Behind all the words and ritual of each Mass is the mystery of being sent in the mission of Jesus. Being sent by Jesus and with Jesus is part of every eucharist we celebrate.

Jesus, sent by the Father, we walk with you.
Jesus, sent by the Father, we suffer with you.
Jesus, sent by the Father, gather us in joy.

Saturday of the 6th Week of Easter TO BE RECONCILED

In sending his disciples, Jesus invites them to the ministry of forgiveness of sins. All of us can be ministers of forgiveness in the way we invite others into the world of forgiveness. Each time we forgive someone, the world of forgiveness is created anew, and the environment of forgiveness is wider. Each time we accept another's forgiveness, or efforts towards forgiveness, the light of forgiveness brightens some darkness. We realise it is difficult to forgive; perhaps it is one of life's most difficult tasks. The example of Jesus is challenging us, for the invitation to forgive is made on the cross, and moments of sacramental forgiveness highlight in a sure way this environment of forgiveness, which is the environment of God.

Lord, may I know I am forgiven.
May I want to forgive others.
Lord, have mercy.

Sunday of the 7th Week of Easter **LOVE: HUMAN AND DIVINE**

Wherever love between two people is found, God is present. In all forms of love – friendships, family, parent-child, husband-wife – God is found in that space of relationship which is truly love. In the space where people really make room for each other and care for another beyond care for self, that is the space of God in human love. Romantic love has its space for God, as does friendship, marriage and family. The space of love between two people is a sacred space and the ground of their love is holy ground. The space of love, no matter who the people are, is to be respected as something so sacred that little else, except the love of God, should interfere with it.

Spirit of love, move among us.
Spirit of love, be joy among us.
Spirit of love be hope and delight.

Monday of the 7th Week of Easter **LOVE: HUMAN AND DIVINE**

Are we not often unaware of much that is under our noses? People who live in the shadow of beautiful scenery often scarcely notice it. Others say that not a day passes but they enjoy the view over the sea and mountains. Love can be like that. We get used to it, live with it, but may not enjoy it or see its link to God. All human love is the creation of God, and is being continually created in the circle of the love of the Father, Son and Spirit. All love is a gateway to the life of the risen Lord. This does not take away from the beauty of human love of itself, but links it to the beauty of the Divine. Love is beautiful: God is beauty.

Love divine, all love excelling,
Spirit of love, of Father and Son,
be present in our human love.

Tuesday of the 7th Week of Easter GIVING LOVE

It's a deep human need to want love – to love and be loved. Many a celibate person will say that a sacrifice in celibacy, as well as not being specially loved by someone, is that they have nobody to love in that way. There is a desire in the human heart to reach out to give of our best to another, to be generous and to take satisfaction in saying, 'I have given love.' At a death-bed I heard a mother of a large family saying in a whisper over and over again, 'I tried my best to love you all.' There's often a searing pain in giving love, especially if we feel rejected, but it's true to say that we come back again and again to wanting to give in love. This is something like the love of Jesus, and it is the life of the Spirit of God.

Be with me, Lord in my giving,
be with me in generosity,
be with me in my loving.

Wednesday of the 7th Week of Easter UNCONDITIONAL LOVE

There's something in each of us that wants to be unconditionally loved. The child symbolises that for us: a child can be looking at us, playing for us, and saying, without words but in every other way, 'love me just as I am'. We look for that often in human friendships, marriage and other relationships. We need to hear in the depths of our sense of ourselves, the words, 'You are loved.' We get this partially in human love and fully in God. The love of the risen Jesus is not tied by place, or time, or body. The spirit of Jesus is the risen Spirit, breathing the love of God wherever the Spirit moves. Neither is this love tied down by human faults and failings, past life or self-esteem. It is total and unconditional love for each person. Hard to believe sometimes, but true.

Risen Lord, breathe your love among us.
Risen Lord, breathe your Spirit of love among us.
Risen Lord, breathe your unconditional love among us.

Thursday of the 7th Week of Easter LOVE IS DARK

Love can be dark. Times when we mistrust another's love and cannot stretch our love. Love is tested. Times when we just want to be loved and fail to love, make us doubt love. Love makes us very vulnerable. Real intimacy with another means we enter into a new intimacy with ourselves, and see sides of ourselves we don't like. And then we think the other doesn't like these either. Real intimacy exposes our weaknesses to another and we can feel almost naked and mistrustful of ourselves. This darkness of love brings us face to face with an essential reality of love – that love is built on faith. If we really love someone then we believe in him or her, and believe in ourselves. This faith is tested in the darkness of love, and within that darkness we find the light of love.

Risen Lord, build our love on faith.
Build our faith on trust in you.
May we walk the path of love with you.

Friday of the 7th Week of Easter MEMORIES OF LOVE

Some of the deepest memories in life have to do with love we have seen or experienced. We can remember back to childhood and remember lessons of love from people who selflessly cared for a sick child or parent, who treated the poor with respect and dignity, who cared for the things of God. If we are touched by love, it goes deep and we may remember it at a time when we need to know the security of love. What we can be most grateful for in life is the memory of love we have received ourselves. Parents, friends, spouse, children – all give us wellsprings of hope and security that bring us a joy in life, and beat for us a path to the doorway of God.

Jesus, lover of your people, be close to us.
Jesus, risen in the love of the Father, be close to us.
Jesus, giver of the Spirit of love, be close to us.

Saturday of the 7th Week of Easter ACTIONS NOT WORDS

We look for the proof of love and want more than words or poems or songs. We judge a person's love on what is done for others. Jesus' 2000 year gift of love was love until death. There is no arguing with the love that puts itself out for others. Parents do it every day, as do many others. As we get closer to God we do it more readily. When the love of God is the air we breathe, we respond more readily in love. Prayer, and any sort of contact with God, is what feeds our desire for love into action of love. Our love in action is often the simple word, the helping hand, the compassionate attitude, the look that gives hope and acceptance, and the willingness to look out for those in need. The Spirit of love says to us that whatever we do for the least of God's people, we do in love for God.

Spirit of love, breathe into our lives.
Spirit of friendship, draw us closer to friends.
Spirit of the universe, make our love universal.